The Gift of Saint Benedict

INTRODUCED BY VERNA A. HOLYHEAD SGS
ILLUSTRATED BY LYNNE MUIR

ave maria press Notre Dame, IN

Published in the U.S.A. by Ave Maria Press, Notre Dame, Indiana 46556

International Standard Book Number: 0-87793-983-7

Illustrations: Copyright © 2002 Lynne Muir
Compilation and introductions: Copyright © 2002 Verna A. Holyhead SGS

www.avemariapress.com

First published 2002
Design, illustration and typesetting by Lynne Muir
Printed by Tien Wah Press, Singapore
Published in the United States by arrangement with John Garratt Publishing, Australia

The National Library of Australia
Cataloguing-in-Publication data

   Holyhead, Verna.
        The gift of St Benedict.

        Bibliography.
        ISBN 1 875938 92 3.

        1. Benedict, Saint, Abbot of Monte Cassino. 2. Benedict,
        Saint, Abbot of Monte Cassino - Meditations. 3. Christian
        life - Meditations. I. Muir, Lynne, 1955- . II. Title.

        242

Quotations from *The Rule of St. Benedict* are from *Benedict's Rule. A Translation and Commentary* by Terrence G. Kardong, published by The Liturgical Press, Collegeville, Minnesota, 1996 and reproduced by permission of the publishers.

CONTENTS

INTRODUCTION

For over fifteen hundred years, many men and women have sought to live more creatively by drawing from the wisdom of *The Rule of Benedict*. That this ancient text has survived so long as a spiritual guide affirms its enduring value.

Benedict was born about 480 into a Roman family in the Italian town of Norcia. Sent as a young man to study in Rome, he was scandalized and disillusioned by the conduct of his fellow students, and fled that city to join for a time with a group of men who were trying devoutly to live the gospel. Helped by the monk Romanus, Benedict then became a hermit for several years in a cave at Subiaco, about 75 km north east of Rome. Eventually, he was discovered by shepherds who recognized his holiness and spread the word about him. Soon Benedict was the centre of attention, visitors came to him for spiritual guidance, and communities of his disciples were established along the steep slopes. To maintain peace when a local priest became jealous of Benedict, he and some of his disciples left Subiaco for the town of Cassino. Within the walls of the ancient fortress on the summit of its mountain, Benedict established a new community. He died at Monte Cassino and was buried there beside his twin sister, Scholastica, who had followed him into the monastic life.

Like our own, Benedict's was an age that witnessed great change: wars, the collapse of the Roman Empire, and social and economic insecurity which widened the gap between rich and poor. Within the church there was turmoil and controversy about faith issues.

The temptation in times of change can be to withdraw nostalgically behind the barricades of the past, or to storm headlong into the future. Benedict was seduced by neither option. He chose a middle way, a lifestyle in which he tried to hold in dynamic balance both individual differences and commitment to community, work and prayer, nature and grace. It is this way of life that he writes about in 'this modest Rule for beginners'. Benedict originally wrote his Rule for men, but more important is the hope that readers will recognize its wisdom as inclusive of women who for centuries have lived and adapted it to the feminine.

Beyond the monastery, the Rule has ecumenical appeal for those who feel a longing for an often undefined something more. We may live physically close in our neighborhoods, our workplaces, our cities, yet there, and even in our families, we often seem to be strangers to one another. Perhaps we hope for a seachange which will sweep us out of loneliness into some harbor of silence and stillness where we are no longer pulled apart and alienated from ourselves and our world, and can drop anchor in God.

Benedict's starting point is always the word of God. His Rule is written to help his followers scrutinize their lives through the prism of scripture. It is best read, therefore, in the way that scripture is read, as 'sacred reading' or *lectio divina*.

The Rule is like an old, full-bodied red wine; it is best enjoyed in sips. A person who exceeds moderation, or does not know how to drink with discernment, is to be pitied. Head and heart, soul and spirit ought to relish the words of the

5

Rule, just as the eye is gladdened at the colour of wine, while the tongue, sense of smell and palate – each in its own way – savour the precious gift of God. If one has tasted on the tongue a maxim of Benedict's by repeating it over and over to oneself, one will reflect further, follow it up by meditating on biblical words, parables or characters which suggest themselves to us, or by meditating on the Person, the mystery, and the teaching of Jesus. This is the 'meditation method' of the ancient Church of East and West; it will open out again and again into a spontaneous prayer. [1]

This book offers only some first sips of Benedict's good wine. On the last page are suggestions for drinking more deeply.

Just as the eye is gladdened by the color of wine, so it will be excited by Lynne Muir's beautiful calligraphy and illumination. For centuries the sons and daughters of Benedict labored with love in their scriptoria, transforming the raw material of vellum, parchment and inks into pages of beauty that reverenced and shared the holy words that they wrote. Lynne is a worthy heir to this tradition. She adds a dimension of 'visual *lectio*' which encourages us to gaze as well as read.

Verna A Holyhead SGS
Melbourne, 21 March 2002

---

1 *The Rule of Benedict: A Guide to Christian Living*, with Commentary by George Holzherr. Translated by Monks of Glenstal Abbey, Dublin, Four Courts Press, 1982, p.2.

mobility rather than stability is a characteristic of much contemporary life. We move to second, third or more careers, we buy and sell and move house more frequently; business people may take intercapital plane flights several times a week; the phones we carry are mobile. But what is significant for our spiritual life is the restlessness of spirit that is a familiar experience for many. *Acedia* was the name given by the ancient and wise monastic writers to this restless living.

St Stephen Harding said that stability is 'to be a lover of the Rule and of the place', and to allow oneself to be formed by these until death. For the women and men who profess this vow, it does not necessarily mean lifelong physical stability in one monastery, although for some communities the latter is their particular expression of the Rule. Whatever the external expression of stability, the most important aspect of this promise is always the deeper stability of heart, the commitment to a continuing search for God in a particular way of life, and a readiness to sink one's personal roots deep into a community, standing firm with its members in the concrete realities of everyday life.

These realities of course will change, and so paradoxically the vow of stability is also a promise to accept change. Benedict encourages his monks to listen every day to the new 'today' of God's voice. He quotes the Matthean parable of the wise person whose house remained strong and secure through flood, wind and storm, because it was built on rock. Those for whom the word of God is the foundation of their lives will withstand life's battering.

On the edge of an Australian city, the bodies of more than a hundred street kids who found no security, no gentleness, no purpose in life, lie in a cemetery under mounds of red earth. Nothing marks their graves, just a warning about snakes and a few rabbit burrows in a stretch of dry, cracked earth. They were homeless in life, unnamed and unclaimed even in death. For them, 'home' was about relationships denied, abused, seduced. 'Who am I?', and 'Where am I?' are related questions. Unanswered they can have tragic results. Stability well lived can witness to the significance and possibility of belonging, which so many people, both young and old, are seeking.

The newcomer to the monastery was required to run the gauntlet of a year's perseverance and patience while his potential for the life was mutually discerned by the community and himself. For Benedict, perseverance is another definition of stability: an ability to keep on going through the desert stretches of our lives, firstly, by abiding in the God of steadfast love who is committed to the world in Christ and, secondly, through the encouraging companionship of those who take up the cross of Christ daily and follow him.

Stability demands patience with oneself, with others, with God. It is an active waiting like that of a pregnant woman who is 'expectant', hopeful, ready to suffer birth pangs for the joy of bringing a new life into the world. The truly patient monk, says Benedict, will certainly share in the sufferings of Christ, but will also experience the joy of new birth… into his kingdom.

The one to be received (into the monastery),
however,
must first promise his stability, fidelity to the
monastic life and obedience
before all in the oratory.

If we wish to dwell in the tent of his kingdom
we shall not arrive
unless we run there by good deeds.

THE RULE OF ST BENEDICT Prol 33

Thus the Lord says in the Gospel:
'Whoever hears my words and does them
I liken to a prudent person who built a house on a rock.
The floods came, the winds blew and battered that house,
but it did not collapse because it was founded on rock'
(Matt 7: 24–25).

dwell

But as we progress in the monastic life and in faith,
our hearts will swell with
the unspeakable sweetness of love,
enabling us to run the way of God's commandments.
Then we will never depart from his teaching
and we will persevere in his doctrine
in the monastery until death.
Likewise, we will participate in the passion of Christ
through patience
so as to deserve to be companions in his kingdom.

habitare

They should bear each other's weaknesses
of both body and character
with the utmost patience.

The workshop where we should work hard
in all these things
is the monastic enclosure and
stability in the community.

STABILITY

THE RULE OF ST BENEDICT 7.42

Moreover, those who maintain patience
in the face of setbacks and injustices
fulfill the command of the Lord:
When they are slapped on the cheek,
they present the other one as well.
When someone takes their shirt,
they give up their coat as well.
Pressed into service for one mile, they go two.

STABILITAS

DWELL

THE RULE OF ST BENEDICT 58.9

If he (the one seeking admission to the community)
promises to persevere in his stability,
after a period of two months
let this Rule be read to him straight through.

HABITARE

Conversion

The second Benedictine promise means much more than our common understanding of 'conversion' as a turning away from or to some ideology, religion, or opinion. The more accurate terminology of the Rule is *conversatio morum*: fidelity to a way of life and behaviour in a community that is on the move, constantly turning and being turned to God through the gift of divine grace. Stability, *conversatio* and obedience ebb and flow together.

Any monastic or married golden jubilarian knows how vast the difference is between first love and love tested by fifty years of relationship. A personal wisdom and freedom have developed which discern the essential from the inessential; the rhythms of individual lives and loves have not been abolished but synchronized; differences which are no threat to the relationship are not so much debated as lovingly tolerated and respected. How this happens is perhaps summed up in the answer given by a monk when asked what he and his community did all day. He replied, 'We go on and fall down and get up; and go on and fall down and get up…'.

Paul told his church at Rome: 'Do not be conformed to this world, but be transformed by the renewing of your minds, so that you may discern what is the will of God – what is good and acceptable and perfect' (Rom 12: 2). When Benedict tells his monks to be strangers to the world, like Paul, he is not recommending contempt for the world, which would run contrary to the mystery of the incarnation and the mission of the church to humanize the world and make it ready to be a new creation under the rule of God. He asks, rather, that his followers discern and dis-own the 'world' of anything which separates them from or takes prece-dence over the love of Christ, all that misdirects them from the guidance of the gospel or abuses our humanity. The monk is to long for the heav-enly city 'with the desire of the Spirit', and his *conversatio* or way of life is to give a radical and human witness to the goal of the journey of all the baptized, a witness that is not disembodied or aloof, but at the heart of the church and world.

In his chapter on the observance of Lent (and nowhere else), Benedict twice uses the word 'joy': joy of the Holy Spirit, and the joy of spiritual longing for Holy Easter, which he wishes to permeate not just the season of Lent, but the whole of the monk's life.

The Desert Mother, Amma Syncletica said:

Great endeavours and hard struggles await those who are converted, but afterwards inexpressible joy. If you want to light a fire you are troubled at first by smoke, and your eyes pour water. But in the end you achieve your aim. Now it is written: 'Our God is a consuming fire'. So we must light the divine fire in us with tears and struggle.

Our God who is a consuming fire is often as unpredictable as one. Conversion of a life to such a God must be ready for the wind of the Spirit to change what was thought to be the right and safe direction; to surprise with revelations of both personal and communal strengths and weak-nesses; and to encourage disciplined learning in 'the school of the Lord's service'… until death.

THE RULE OF ST BENEDICT Prol 20-21

Look, the Lord in his devotion to us
shows us the way to life.
Therefore, let us belt our waist with faith
that leads to the performance of good works.
Let us set out on this path
with the gospel as our guide
so that we may be worthy to see him
who has called us into his kingdom.

…we must run and accomplish now
what will profit us for eternity.
Therefore we must establish a school
for the Lord's service.
In its organization we have tried not to create
anything grim or oppressive.
In a given case we may have to
arrange things a bit strictly
to correct vice or preserve charity.
When this happens, do not immediately
take fright and flee the path of salvation,
which can only be narrow at its outset.

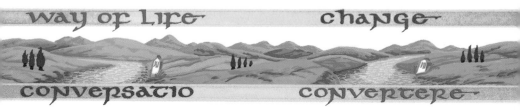

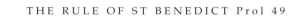

THE RULE OF ST BENEDICT Prol 49

But as we progress in the monastic life and in faith,
our hearts will swell with
the unspeakable sweetness of love,
enabling us to race along
the ways of God's commandments.

CONVERSATIO

THE RULE OF ST BENEDICT 49.1,6-7

At all times the lifestyle of a monk ought to
have a Lenten quality…
each one, of his own free will,
with the joy of the Spirit,
can offer God something
beyond what is imposed on him…
Let him await Holy Easter
with the joy of spiritual desire.

CONVERTERE

You should become a stranger to the world's ways.
Prefer nothing to the love of Christ.

When someone comes first to the monastic life,
he should not be allowed entry too readily,
but as the Apostle says:
'Test whether the spirits be godly' (1 Jn 4: 1).

THE RULE OF ST BENEDICT 58.24-26

If he has possessions,
he should give them to the poor beforehand,
or he should give them to the monastery
by a gift made in solemn form.
He must keep nothing at all back for himself,
since he knows that from henceforward
he does not even have any more power
even over his own body.
So then and there in the oratory
he should be stripped of the clothes he is wearing
and clothed in the garb of the monastery.

THE RULE OF ST BENEDICT 73.1-5

… what page or even what word of the
divinely inspired Old and New Testaments
is not a completely reliable guidepost
for human life?
Or what book of the holy Catholic Fathers does not teach
us how to reach our Creator by the direct route.
And then there are the Conferences of the Fathers
and their Institutes and Lives,
along with the Rule of our holy Father Basil.

In contemporary life we may seem to spend much of our time listening. but often this may only take us across the threshold of 'auditory overload' into a kind of mindless noise.

Benedict begins his Rule with the word: 'Listen', a listening with 'the ear of the heart'. To listen (*obaudire*) is to obey, and obedience is the third promise which a Benedictine professes. It is, firstly, a call to hear and respond to the word of God. This word is most explicit in the Word made flesh, Jesus Christ, and in his good news. It is to him that Benedict summons his followers to return by the 'labor of obedience' by taking up the 'powerful and shining weapons of obedience' in order to fight for and establish God's reign over the territory of the human heart.

To a society that values collaboration, consultation, and team ministry, Benedict has much to offer. He recognizes the significance of listening to our sisters and brothers through whom the call of God also comes. Not only obedience to the leader of the community, the abbot, but mutual obedience of its members, one to the other, is called 'a blessing', an acknowledgment that everyone has some wisdom, and no one has it all. Benedict stresses that whenever important matters are to be decided, the abbot must call together the whole community and ask for the counsel of each one, even and especially the youngest. All must tune the ears of their hearts to the Rule and not be arrogant, prejudiced or deaf to each other's words. Although the decision rests with the abbot, right judgment requires him to ponder the counsel offered.

Fear-filled, grudging obedience or obedience eroded by subtle murmuring, is not the obedience of those who hold nothing dearer to them than Christ and his obedience.

There is a tough practicality about Benedictine obedience. If what seems an impossible is asked, the monk should listen to his interior conflict. The Rule gives the right to speak out of this to the superior in well-timed, patient and respectful dialogue. The last word, however, may be 'obey' – with trust in the loving and special help of God for the weak.

Obedience will never be possible without interior silence; not the silence which is a rehearsal of what we will say when someone else stops talking, but the contemplative silence which ponders the word.

Etty Hillesum, a young Jewish woman who died in Auschwitz in 1943, wrote in her diary a year earlier:

> Truly, my life is one long hearkening unto myself and others, unto God. And if I say that I hearken, it is really God who hearkens inside me. The most essential and the deepest in me hearkening to the most essential and deepest in the other. God to God.[2]

Not many will achieve that degree of listening by Etty's age of twenty-nine but, says Benedict, it gets easier. Good listeners become good runners. Paced by Jesus Christ over the course of a lifetime, our hearts expand and beat strongly 'with the unspeakable sweetness of love', and we race along the way of God's commandments to cross the finishing line of death and receive the prize of the kingdom.

2 *Etty: A Diary 1941-43*, London, Triad Grafton Books, 1985, p.224.

Listen, O my son, to the teachings of your master,
and turn to them with the ear of your heart.
Willingly accept the advice of a devoted father
and put it into action.
Thus you will return by the labor of obedience
to the one from whom you drifted
through the inertia of disobedience.
Now then I address my words to you:
whoever is willing to renounce self-will and take up
the powerful and shining weapons of obedience
to fight for the Lord Christ, the true king.

'Whoever has ears for hearing should listen
to what the Spirit says to the churches' (Rev 2: 7).

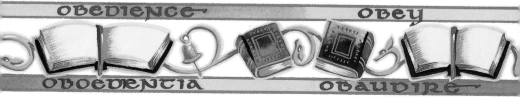

THE RULE OF ST BENEDICT 7.57-58

Scripture shows that
In much talk one does not escape sin,
and *the chatterbox does not walk straight on the earth.*

THE RULE OF ST BENEDICT 3.1-3

As often as important questions
have to be dealt with in the monastery,
the abbot should convene the whole community
and himself tell them what is involved.
When he has heard the advice of the brothers,
let him ponder the matter and
then do what he thinks best.
Now the reason why we said
that all are to be convened
is that the Lord often reveals
what is best to the youngest.

OBAUDIRE

The basic road to progress for the humble person
is through prompt obedience.
This is characteristic of those who hold
Christ more precious than all else.

… they prefer to walk according to the
judgment and command of another,
living in cenobitic community with an abbot over them.
Doubtless, people such as these
imitate the Lord, who said:
'I did not come to do my own will,
but the will of the one who sent me'…
Obedience given to superiors is given to God,
who said:
'Whoever listens to you, listens to me.'

OBEDIENCE

But if he sees that the weight of the task
altogether exceeds his strength,
he should patiently point out to the superior
why he cannot do it.
He should do this at the proper time,
and without pride, obstinacy or refusal…
Then confident in the love of God,
he must lovingly obey.

OBOEDIENTIA

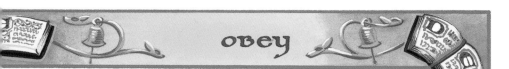

THE RULE OF ST BENEDICT 71.1-2

The blessing of obedience
is not only something that everyone
ought to show the abbot,
but the brothers should also obey one another.
They know they will go to God
by this path of obedience.

OBAUDIRE

humility and humanity both derive from the Latin *humus*, earth, soil. Humility is a grounding in one's humanity, an acceptance of our place in the universe and a refusal to succumb to the primeval temptation – to be like God. Chapter 7 is, therefore, basically a chapter about right relationships.

Benedict's frequent reference to scripture in nearly every verse of this chapter underlines the fact that he gives priority to attentive listening to the word of God for understanding of and progress in humility. He begins with Jesus' saying: 'All who exalt themselves will be humbled, and those who humble themselves will be exalted' (Lk 14:11; 18:14). Humility is hospitable and makes way for others at the table of life.

He then refers to Jacob's dream (Gen 28: 10–17). The angels ascending and descending the ladder and the presence of God above it made Bethel holy ground for Jacob, and he exclaimed: 'Surely the Lord is in this place – and I did not know it!' Benedict encourages his monks to recognize God's presence on the twelve steps of the ladder of humility stretched between the ground of our humanity and heaven. There God will also be present in situations where we, too, 'did not know it'.

The climb begins with 'fear of the Lord', a reverent mindfulness of God's presence. The monk climbs, seeking the will of God as Christ did, in obedience. The strength for the climb comes from the love of Christ, not from immature dependency or exaggerated submissiveness. Humility is not to be confused with humiliations, but humility offers a way of dealing with humiliations that promotes physical and psychological health. Peace under pressure can come through our following of the suffering servant Christ.

Humble people know that they are not perfect, and so at times they need to open themselves to the liberating and objective wisdom of another. Humility allows pride in a task well done, but without longing for lavish congratulations or status. The challenge of the seventh step is the hard ability to take criticism and avoid judgment of others. In his climb, the monk comes to respect the traditions and experience of the past. Personal initiative is not denied, but not everyone and everything have been waiting for centuries for transformation to an individual's personal preferences. Laughter has its place, but not that which is cynical or cruel.

A brother once asked a wise old monk: 'What is humility?' And the sage answered: 'To do good to those who hurt you.' 'But if you cannot do that, what should you do?' The old man replied: 'Get away from them and keep your mouth shut.'

Few climb without slipping, but the one who lives truthfully will, like the tax collector at prayer in the temple, be able to descend into personal limitations and sinfulness, find God there, and resume the climb. Gradually the heart will be revealed even in external behavior. The last step brings the monk to the perfect love of Christ that casts out fear (cf.1 Jn 4: 18) and is a gift of the Holy Spirit. So Benedict ends this chapter as he began: under obedience to and encouragement of the word of God.

Brothers, the Holy Scripture cries out to us, saying:
Whoever is self-promoting will be humbled,
and whoever is humble will be promoted.

…we must set up that ladder
which appeared to Jacob in a dream.
It showed him angels descending and ascending.
Doubtless we should understand
this descent and ascent as follows:
one descends by pride and ascends by humility.
The towering ladder is, of course, our earthly life.
When the heart is humble, God raises it up to heaven.
We could say that our body and soul
are the sides of this ladder,
into which the divine summons has inserted
various rungs of humility and discipline for the ascent.

humility

THE RULE OF ST BENEDICT 7.65-66

He should always repeat in his heart what
the publican said in the gospel,
his eyes cast downward:
*Lord, I am a sinner and not worthy
to raise my eyes to heaven.*
And also with the Prophet:
I am bowed down and totally humbled.

humilitas

THE RULE OF ST BENEDICT 7.67

Therefore, when he has climbed
all these steps of humility,
the monk will soon arrive at
that perfect love of God which drives out fear.

humanitas

The brothers, however,
should offer their advice to the abbot
with all deference and humility,
and not presume to assert their views
in a bold manner.

The basic road to progress for the humble person
is through prompt obedience.

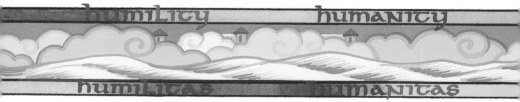

THE RULE OF ST BENEDICT 31.7,13-14

If some brother should demand something
from him (the cellarer) in an unreasonable way,
he should not crush him with a rebuke,
but deny the obnoxious petitioner
in a reasonable and humble manner.
… above all else he should have humility,
and when he has no material goods
to give someone who asks,
he should at least return a friendly word.
For it is written:
A good *word is better than the best gift.*

humilitas

Let them love their abbot
with sincere and humble charity.

The significance of Benedictine community is beautifully and ritually expressed during the ceremony for the admission of a brother to the community as described in Chapter 58 of the Rule. Immediately after the novice has placed on the altar a copy of his promises written in his own hand, he sings verse 116 of Ps 119: 'Receive me, Lord, according to your promise and I will live. Do not disappoint me in my hope.' Three times this is sung, and three times the community repeats it, the last time adding the 'Glory be' in praise of the Trinity, the icon of every community. The brother then prostrates at the feet of each member of the community. Symbolically, he throws himself on the mercy of God present in his brothers. These are the ones with whom he will abide, through whom he will be encouraged or disappointed in seeking God. His own life will twine with each of theirs as branches of a vine. Love of Jesus, the True Vine will grow as the monks tangle their lives with one another. And through the other members of the community God will do much of the pruning of the newly professed in the years ahead.

Antoine de Saint-Exupery's words are often quoted: 'Love is not a matter of looking at each other, but of looking together in the same direction.' Benedict reminds his communities that, with all their diversity, the one direction in which they must always look is the love of Christ and the guidance of his gospel. For constancy in this direction-setting and traveling, the teaching role of the abbot is important. He does this more by doing and less by talking. N only the abbot, but the whole community is reminded that God waits patiently for translation of words into actions.

Benedict believes that one of the most insidious destroyers of community is murmuring or grumbling: that pervasive peevishness that feels almost obliged to be negative and vocal about everyone and everything.

Benedict has strong words to say about 'the vice of private ownership'. He recognizes that material goods are required for work, study, personal ministry and health, but his ideal is the early Christian community's communion of goods. Because they were of one heart and mind, everything was held in common, and needs were met as they arose. There is to be no acquisitiveness or proprietorship with regard not only to material goods, but also in human relationships. The latter destroys the possibility of a healthy sub-culture of friendship which monastic writers affirm as reflecting the relationship between Jesus and his disciples whom he ultimately named as friends (Jn 15: 15).

'The Good Zeal That Monks Ought To Have' (Ch 72) is a praise of love which is warm, reverent, patient and selfless: for one another, for God, for the abbot, for Christ. But if one expects this to mean constant highs in community relationships, as in any other human relationships, the inevitable lows will be much more painful. Realistic love acknowledges that 'bitter zeal' can also be present, and that there will be weaknesses of body and character to be borne with down-to-earth patience. In the end, it is preference for absolutely nothing but Christ that will lead us to everlasting life.

THE RULE OF ST BENEDICT 58.22

… the brother novice should lie prostrate at the feet of
each one (of the community)
so they might pray for him.

Furthermore, when someone accepts the title of abbot,
he should direct his disciples by a twofold teaching.
That means he should demonstrate everything that is
good and holy by his deeds more than his words.

THE RULE OF ST BENEDICT 4.62

Do not wish to be holy before you really are;
first be holy, and then the term
will be true in your case.

accept

THE RULE OF ST BENEDICT 4.39

Do not be a loafer, nor a grumbler,
nor one who runs down the reputation of another.

suscipe

If a disciple obeys grudgingly and murmurs
not only out aloud but internally,
even if he carries out the order,
it will not be acceptable to God.
For he sees the heart of the murmurer,
who will receive no thanks for such a deed.
On the contrary if he does not make satisfaction,
he will receive the penalty of murmurers.

Let all things be common to all, as Scripture says,
so that no one may presume *to call anything his own.*

COMMUNION

THE RULE OF ST BENEDICT 72.4-5

'Let them strive to be the first to honor one another.'
They should bear each other's
weaknesses of both body and character
with the utmost patience.

communio

accept

THE RULE OF ST BENEDICT 72.8-12

They must show selfless love to the brothers.
Let them fear God out of love.
They should love their abbot
with sincere and humble charity.
Let them prefer absolutely nothing to Christ,
and may he lead us all to everlasting life.

suscipe

Prayer

mindfulness of God's presence in the monk's life, and the need to respond to this both communally and personally is the basis of Benedict's simple yet profound approach to prayer. The relationship between communal and personal prayer is that of mutual nourishment. Fasting, bingeing, or fastidious nibbling does not belong in anyone's prayer life, especially one centred primarily on the biblical word.

In the cosmos and our own bodies there are rhythms: of the seasons, of night and day, sleeping and waking, birthing and dying. Prayer also needs rhythm. Our own inner world can be *tohu* and *bohu*, 'unformed and void' (Gen 1: 1) unless the word of God moves regularly over its depths. Benedict the realist knew that this required some structure, so he called his community seven times a day to the Work of God (the Divine Office or Liturgy of the Hours). His delightful humanity is shown in his concern for adequate sleep, digestion and toileting mixed in with his first instructions about the celebration of this liturgical prayer.

In its own particular way, the monastic life is deeply inserted into the world. The Liturgy of the Hours is a repeated reminder to the monk of his responsibility to share in redeeming the world's time by making his heart and voice available to God as a channel of grace for the world. When the Hours are prayed in common, each member of the community is a concrete reminder to the others of the need to be shaken out of one's small, private world into awareness of the tears and joys of others, near or far, known or unknown. The monastic community's communal prayer concretizes this insight for the whole church.

As an observant Jew, the psalms were central to Christ's prayer, as they are to the Work of God. For those who are to prefer nothing whatever to Christ, psalmody therefore has a privileged place in their prayer.

The monk should pray humbly, with a focused heart, 'on target' for God, who has first targeted him and jabbed his heart into awareness of the voice of the Lord inviting him and showing him the way to life.

God is also sought in *lectio divina*, or sacred reading. Its frequent mention in Chapter 48, 'The Daily Manual Labor', underlines Benedict's concern for a balance between liturgy, *lectio*, labor and leisure. *Lectio divina* is not reading for information, but for formation – by God. It is a significant aspect of 'listening' to God by dwelling in and on the text in conversation with our lives. At times our response will be in the 'new language' of deep, attentive silence.

Gradually the word becomes so ingrained in the monk's undivided heart that it pulses through the whole of his day. The word of God is at home in such a heart which is a place of prayer as simple and uncluttered as the monastic oratory.

> One day the Rabbi Baal Shem Tov stopped on the threshold of a synagogue and refused to go in. 'I cannot go in,' he said. 'It is crowded with teachings and prayers from wall to wall and floor to ceiling. How could there be room for me?' When he saw that his companions did not understand what he meant, he added, 'The many words from the lips of those whose teaching and praying do not come from hearts lifted to heaven cannot rise, but fill the house.'

We believe that God is present everywhere and that
the eyes of the Lord
gaze everywhere on the good and bad.
We should, though, be totally convinced that this is so
when we are present at the Divine Office.

And let us stand to sing (the psalms) in such a way
that our mind is in harmony with our voice.

THE RULE OF ST BENEDICT 20.1-2

When we wish to propose something
to powerful people,
we do not presume to do so
without humility and reverence.
How much more should we petition
the Lord God of the universe
with great humility and total devotion.

Lectio Divina

We should also realize that it is not in much talking
that we shall be heard,
but in purity of heart and tearful compunction.
Therefore prayer should be short and pure,
unless perhaps it be prolonged
under the inspiration of divine grace.
But in community, prayer should be very brief…

… nothing should be preferred to the Work of God.
One must note whether he (the novice)
really seeks God,
and whether he is serious about the Work of God,
obedience and hardships.

Idleness is the soul's enemy,
so therefore at determined times
the brothers ought to be occupied with manual labor,
and again at determined times in *lectio divina.*

SACRED READING

THE RULE OF ST BENEDICT 52.1

The oratory should be in fact what it is called,
and nothing else should be done or stored there.

LECTIO DIVINA

When the Work of God is finished,
they should all leave in deepest silence
and show reverence to God.
Thus will the brother who may wish to pray by himself
not be hindered by the thoughtlessness of another.
But if someone perhaps wishes
to pray privately at some time,
let him simply go in and pray, not in a loud voice
but with tears and full attention of heart.

Work

here is a story of Desert Wisdom:

It was told about John the Little that one day he said to his older brother, 'I want to be free from care and not to work but to worship God without interruption.' And he took his robe off, and went into the desert. After staying there one week, he returned to his brother. And when he knocked at the door, his brother asked without opening it, 'Who is it?' He replied, 'It's John, your brother.' The brother said to John, 'John has become an angel and is not among people any more.' Then he begged and said, 'It's me!' But his brother did not open the door and left him there in distress until the next morning. And he finally opened the door and said, 'If you are a human being, you have to work again in order to live.' Then John repented, saying, 'Forgive me, brother, for I was wrong.'

Like John the Little, we cannot opt out of work, but many are longing for a way to be more genuinely human at work. Employers and employees alike are attracted by the wisdom, balance and humanity of Benedict's Rule. For centuries, his monks have tried to work, study, pray, and relate with love and respect for one another, for those in authority, and for the environment. Benedict has no time for pseudo-contemplatives who are so busy finding God in esoteric 'experiences' that they miss God in the everyday, nor for the workaholics.

What Benedict expects of the abbot as steward of the monastic household makes a useful checklist for workplace managers. He should strive to be loved rather than feared, not because he tries to agree with everyone (a sure cause of dissension!), but because of his personal qualities.

He is to be a person of both holy wisdom and holy living, farsighted, well focused, temperate and merciful. In interpersonal relationships, he respects individual differences and matches the worker with the most appropriate work, while remaining aware of corporate needs. The correction of others should be tempered by the acceptance of his own imperfections. Impartial and just, he needs to be able to dialogue, to be flexible and adapt, and in serious decision-making to take counsel as widely as possible. What Benedict has to say about the cellarer, too, is significant for middle managers. But Benedict's communities are not built on a management model. Their foundation is Christ, and whatever the community or individuals build must stand firm and be measured by his life, death and resurrection.

Benedict acknowledges that some monks will have special work skills which are not to be ignored, but they need to be grounded in the remembrance that they are firstly the Lord's workmen. Success at any cost, at the expense of colleagues and clients, would be for Benedict an example of the 'evil and bitter zeal' of contention rather than the 'good zeal' of physical and psychological support of one another.

In the Rule, communal prayer is the Work of God; the monastery is the workshop where the monks handle both the tools of the spiritual craft and those for manual labor; all created things have their own intrinsic worth and are to be esteemed like the sacred vessels of the altar; and there is dignity in working at the most menial task .

The Lord, seeking a worker for himself in the crowds
to whom he calls out, says:
'Which of you desires life and longs to see good days?'
(Ps 34:12).

If, however, the necessities of the place
or poverty demand
that they themselves work at the harvest,
they should not be sad.
For if they live by the work of their hands,
then they are true monks,
as were our Fathers and the apostles.
Yet everything should be arranged in moderation
because of the fainthearted.

WORK TOOLS
LABORARE INSTRUMENTA

Idleness is the soul's enemy,
so therefore at determined times
the brothers ought to be occupied with manual labor,
and again at determined hours in *lectio divina.*

Tools

THE RULE OF ST BENEDICT 4.78

These, then are the tools of the spiritual craft...
The workshop where we should work hard
at all these things
is the monastic enclosure
and stability in the community.

INSTRUMENTA

He (the cellarer) should consider the
pots of the monastery and all its goods
as if they were the holy bowls of the altar.
He must not hold anything as negligible.
Let him not be controlled by avarice,
nor should he waste or dissipate
the goods of the monastery.
He should take a balanced approach to everything,
and follow the abbot's orders.

… the brothers are to be given help when needed,
and whenever they are free,
they work wherever they are assigned.

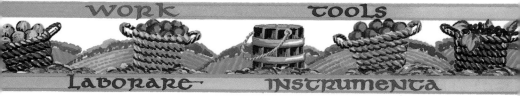

THE RULE OF ST BENEDICT 57.1

If there are skilled workmen in the monastery,
let them practise their crafts
with all humility if the abbot permits.
But if anyone is so proud of his expertise
that he thinks he is
a great gift to the monastery,
he should be removed from his work.
Nor should he return to it
unless he has humbled himself
and the abbot permits it again.

Tools

Once he has been installed,
the abbot must constantly keep in mind
what a burden he has undertaken
and to whom he will have to give
a reckoning of his stewardship (Luke 16: 2).
And he must realize that he must profit others
rather than precede them.

INSTRUMENTA

hospitality

The hospitality Benedict teaches is not a social event but a holy event. It is costly, not in terms of money, but in the demands it makes on our hearts, our time, and our personal resources.

In each of us there is some inner homelessness, some alienation from ourselves and one another which longs for a welcome. Benedict asked his monks to become a shelter to one another, accepting each other with their differences of personality, gifts, and physical resources. Not to extend such a welcome is to remain 'strangers'.

He commences Chapter 53, 'On the Reception of Guests', with the gospel reminder that: 'All guests who arrive should be received as Christ', because in them Christ himself is welcomed. A Benedictine community that does not welcome guests is considered an atypical community.

Our own times know much hostility and loneliness. Benedict's call to his monks to offer a special welcome to pilgrims and the poor can be translated into a call to the wider Christian community for hospitality to those who are both materially disadvantaged or spiritually starved in a world hungry for success at any price. The human faces of these 'guests' may be the faces of political asylum seekers and refugees, unanchored young people, or pilgrims who in so many lifestyles are seeking for an elusive 'something more' that often they themselves cannot name. A listening ear, a quiet place for prayer, a healing space to balance the frenetic clutter of everyday pressures, an environment of simple beauty, these are all aspects of Benedictine hospitality.

Benedict believes that, like Abraham at the oaks of Mamre (Genesis 18), the host is blessed by the guests. When we make hospitality our special care, we may sometimes 'entertain angels without knowing it' (Hebrews 13: 2). So, in annoying disruptions and in demands on our time, we are willing to put aside personal agendas and look for the possibility of welcoming a messenger of God. The person who has no time for others has no time for God.

Hospitality begins in small ways with people of easy approachability, like Benedict's porter: with warmth rather than polite boredom, with friendly words rather than officiousness, with graciousness rather than rudeness, be this at the entrance to the monastery, in families, on the telephone, in the workplace, in our parish church, or in any of the numerous meeting and community situations in our contemporary society.

A reporter in an Indian town at the centre of a violent earthquake once described how he sat beside an old man who had just cremated his wife, killed in the earthquake. With tears streaming down his face, the man offered the reporter some tea. Not even the intensity of that earthquake and a husband's grief, could shake his hospitality. Benedict believed that nothing can shake the ultimate and patient hospitality of God, for we are all guests of the One who has welcomed us into the mystery of life; guests before whom God has spread the lavish feast of creation. We are to respond by moving over, making room, and sharing graciously with our sisters and our brothers.

All guests who arrive should be received as Christ,
for he himself will say,
I was a stranger and you took me in.

So, as soon as a guest is announced,
the superior or the brothers
should hurry to meet them
with every mark of love.
First they should pray together
and then be united in peace.

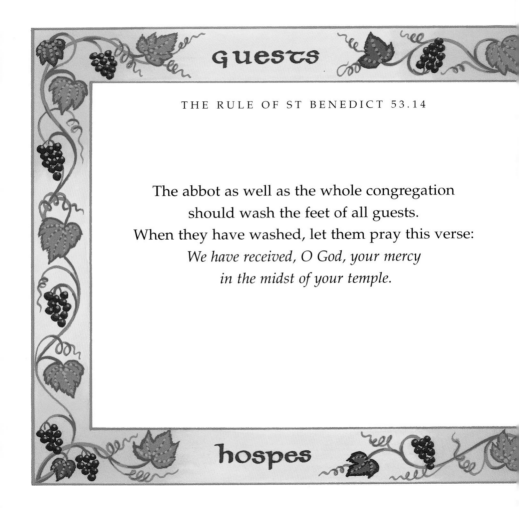

guests

THE RULE OF ST BENEDICT 53.14

The abbot as well as the whole congregation
should wash the feet of all guests.
When they have washed, let them pray this verse:
We have received, O God, your mercy
in the midst of your temple.

hospes

welcome

THE RULE OF ST BENEDICT 53.15

The greatest care should be exhibited
in the reception of the poor and pilgrims,
for Christ is more especially received in them;
for the very fear of the rich wins them respect.

suscipere

A brother full of the fear of God
should be assigned to the guest quarters.
A sufficient number of beds
should be made up there.
And the house of God
should be wisely managed by wise persons.

Above all, he, (the cellarer) should have humility,
and when he has no material goods
to give someone who asks,
he should at least return a friendly word.
For it is written:
A good *word is better than the best gift*.

guests

THE RULE OF ST BENEDICT 66.1

A wise old monk should be stationed
at the gate of the monastery.
He should know how to listen to people
and also how to speak to them...

hospes

welcome

THE RULE OF ST BENEDICT 72.4-5

'Let them strive to be the first
to honor one another.'
They should bear each other's weaknesses
of both body and character
with the utmost patience.

suscipere

Peace is a gift for which we all long. In the Prologue, Benedict urges his community to 'avoid evil and do good', and immediately follows this with the double biblical imperative: 'seek peace and pursue it' (Ps 34: 14). No individual or community ambles mindlessly into peace. The way is by often painful perseverance.

In the face of global war or terrorism we may feel powerless and fearful. Benedict offers us practical, if demanding, ways in which we can confront these evils by creating peace in our own hearts and in our own small worlds of family and community. There is nothing that is in our world that is not first in the human heart.

Benedict describes the seeking and pursuit of peace in social contexts that are easily transplanted outside the monastery. To keep our tongues from evil and our lips from speaking deceit, are the forerunners of the search and pursuit of peace, says Benedict. He is aware of small details of life together, such as the insincere greeting which is at best thoughtlessness and at worst mockery.

Leaders who have to relate to others should be people of peace. In the Rule, this was a special challenge to the abbot and the cellarer, yet the peacemaking qualities of these office holders are applicable to parents, business managers, even politicians! The abbot is not to be a 'turbulent' character or he will not be at peace with himself, and his internal chaos will communicate itself to the community.

Relationships involving material needs or wants, from international politics to supermarket shopping with one's children, can be flash points for peacebreaking. As someone who deals with the material goods of the monastery, the cellarer is not to have an air of proprietorship, but be humble, well-disciplined, and with a tongue that can at least offer a friendly word if there is nothing else he can supply. When necessary, helpers are to be given to him so that he can carry out his duties peacefully, with sensitivity to people and their individual needs.

Allowance for individual needs is important for creating an environment of peace, and Benedict quotes the ideal of the early Christian community where distribution was made: 'to each as any had need' (Acts 4: 34), without fear or favor. Guests, too, are to be united in peace with the community, first by prayer and then by the exchange of a kiss of peace.

Living a non-violent life makes daily demands, so every morning and evening Benedict calls for the Lord's Prayer to be recited in choir. Whether monastic, married, or single, how we say the prayer is much less significant than why we are encouraged to frame our day with the sobering plea to God 'to forgive as we forgive', and so root out the thorns of quarreling which can spring up so quickly and choke love. It is mindfulness of the love of Christ and his overwhelming mercy which enables us to pray for our enemies, or pray to the Father for his forgiveness of them. Where possible, peace is to be made before sunset, or a wounded relationship may fester. And Benedict adds a final word of encouragement when peacemaking seems personally or politically distant: 'Never despair of God's mercy.'

If you desire true and lasting life,
keep your tongue from evil
and your lips from speaking deceit;
avoid evil and do good;
seek peace and pursue it.

Do not give a false peace.

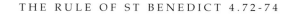
peace

THE RULE OF ST BENEDICT 4.72-74

Pray for your enemies for the love of Christ.
If you have a quarrel with someone,
make peace before sundown.
And never despair of God's mercy.

pax

THE RULE OF ST BENEDICT 13.12-13

This (recitation of the Lord's Prayer) is done
because of the thorns of quarreling
that often spring up.
When the brothers respond to the prayer:
'Forgive as we forgive',
they make a solemn pact
to purge this vice from themselves.

DIMITTERE

(The cellarer) should be a wise person,
of mature character and well disciplined.
He should not be gluttonous, arrogant,
violent, unfair, stingy or wasteful.

If the community is rather large,
let him (the cellarer) be given
helpers to aid him
so he can peacefully perform
the duties entrusted to him.

peace

THE RULE OF ST BENEDICT 34.5

So the one who needs less
should thank God and not be sad.
And whoever needs more
should be humble about his weaknesses,
and not gloat over the mercy shown him.
Thus all the members will be at peace.

pax

FORGIVE

THE RULE OF ST BENEDICT 65.16

(The abbot) should not be restless and troubled,
not extreme and headstrong,
not jealous and oversuspicious;
for then he will have no peace.

DIMITTERE

Compassion

Compassion is the deep, gut wrenching response to and embracing of the situation of another. As a radical critique of blind legalism, cynical indifference, or established subservience, it is a work of justice, which announces that another's dignity or hurt is to be taken seriously. And it is woven into the whole fabric and all seasons of a Benedictine community's life.

The sick, says Benedict, are to be the special care of the community, 'before and above all else.' As Christ is welcomed in the guest, so he is served in the sick with a personal, as well as functional relationship. His approach to the sick is holistic: respectful of their quality of life, the needs of the body, their diet, privacy and appropriate accommodation, but also calling for patient concern when their morale is low. The sick, too, have their own particular challenges to meet and overcome. Petulance, excessive demands or self-centredness, are realistic stumbling stones for the sick disciple.

A statue of the Good Shepherd (c. 60 AD at Caesarea Maritima, Israel) shows only the damaged torso of the shepherd. Around his shoulders is wrapped a ponderously stupid looking sheep, equal in weight to the statue. To allow oneself to be found, and to carry home the found one, are both heavy tasks. As compassionate shepherd and physician, the abbot is to have special concern for those who are soul-sick and wandering from the way of life they have professed. In his relationships with them, he is to enflesh Christ's compassionate action. Chapter 27, with the rather alarming title of 'What the Abbot's Care for the Excommunicated Should Be', has been called one of the most remarkable in the Rule, reflecting as it does both Benedict's realism about and love for sinners. Surrounded with delicate confidentiality, the abbot is to send wise and experienced members of the community with a mission of advice and consolation to the wavering monk. That Benedict does not suggest he go himself, may be a judgment that a less authoritative approach would be more successful.

Authority that is compassionate neither tosses aside the weak nor rules violently over the strong. If a monk must be corrected, the abbot is not to be too vigorous in rubbing away the corrosive 'rust', lest the human vessel be broken. Good pastoral care in any context does not aim to condemn or exclude, but to love, heal and absorb the hurt, even to the extent of the servant shepherd laying down his own life for the sheep. The most important account the cellarer has to keep is his treatment of the vulnerable.

For other 'little ones', the young, the old and the poor in and beyond the community, the Rule adds its own urgency to human concern. Benedict holds up a mirror to our social consciences in which we may see today the need for compassion reflected in tragedies of child abuse and slavery, disregard for the frail aged and people with disabilities, and the emphasis on productivity as an indicator of a person's worth. To help the troubled and console the sorrowful is a tool of good works that all must handle, he says. Perhaps there is no better summary of a compassionate response than the way in which the porter is to greet visitors and the poor: 'quickly…in the warmth of charity.'

Go to help the troubled
and console the sorrowing.

The sick are to be cared for
before and above all else,
for it is really Christ who is served in them.
He himself said:
I was sick and you visited me, and
Whatever you did to one of these little ones,
you did to me.

charity

THE RULE OF ST BENEDICT 37.1-2

While human nature itself is indulgent
toward these two groups,
namely the aged and children,
the authority of the Rule should also
look out for them.

CARITAS

Love

He (the abbot) should understand that he has undertaken
to care for the weak and not to dominate the strong.
Let him fear the threat of the Prophet
by whose mouth God says:
You took for yourselves what you saw was plump,
but the feeble you threw out (Ezek 34: 3–4).
Let him imitate the good shepherd's devoted example...
He was so filled with sympathy at its weakness
that *he* mercifully *placed it on his* sacred *shoulders*
and carried it back to the flock.

Diligere

He (the cellarer) should lavish great care,
on the sick, the children, the guests and the poor,
knowing without any doubt
that he will have to give an account for all these
on judgment day.

He (the abbot) must be learned in the Divine Law
so he will know how to
bring forth both old and new (Matt 13: 52).
He should be chaste, temperate and merciful,
and always *put mercy before judgment* (Jas 2: 13)
so that he himself may obtain the former.

charity

When he must correct someone,
he (the abbot) should act prudently and not overdo it.
If he is too vigorous in removing the rust,
he may break the vessel.
Let him always be wary of his own brittleness,
and remember not to break the bent reed.

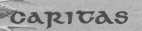
CARITAS

Love

As soon as anyone knocks or a poor person cries out,
he (the porter) should respond
'Thanks be to God!' or 'Bless me!'
Filled with the gentleness of the fear of God,
he must quickly respond with the warmth of charity.

DILIGERE

FOR DRINKING MORE DEEPLY OF
THE WISDOM OF THE RULE OF BENEDICT

RB *1980:The Rule of St Benedict in English*, edited by Timothy Fry OSB, Collegeville, Minnesota, The Liturgical Press, 1982 (Pocket-sized edition).

Joan Chittister OSB, *Wisdom Distilled From the Daily: Living the Rule of St Benedict Today*, San Francisco, Harper and Row, Publishers, 1995.

Esther de Waal, *A Life-giving Way: A Commentary on the Rule of St Benedict*, London, Geoffrey Chapman, 1995.

Demetrius Dumm OSB, *Cherish Christ Above All: The Bible in the Rule of Benedict*, New York/Mahwah, NJ, Paulist Press, 1996.

Katherine Howard OSB, *Praying with Benedict*, Winona, St Mary's Press, 1997.

Columba Stewart OSB, *Prayer and Community: The Benedictine Tradition*, London, Darton, Longman & Todd, 1998.

Norvene Vest, Oblate OSB, *Preferring Christ: A Devotional Commentary and Workbook on the Rule of St Benedict*, Trabuco Canyon CA, Source Books CA/ Wheathampstead Herts., Anthony Clarke Books, 1990.